9011862848

RE...WED
APR 2024

KU-020-055

Let's Get Mapping!

Mapping Information

EAST RIDING
OF YORKSHIRE COUNCIL
Schools Library Service

PROJECT
June 2014

Melanie Waldron

Raintree is an imprint of Capstone Global Library Limited, a company incorporated in England and Wales having its registered office at 7 Pilgrim Street, London, EC4V 6LB – Registered company number: 6695582

To contact Raintree please phone 0845 6044371, fax + 44 (0) 1865 312263, or email myorders@ raintreepublishers.co.uk. Customers from outside the UK please telephone +44 1865 312262.

Text © Capstone Global Library Limited 2013
First published in hardback in 2013
First published in paperback in 2014
The moral rights of the proprietor have been asserted.

All rights reserved. No part of this publication may be reproduced in any form or by any means (including photocopying or storing it in any medium by electronic means and whether or not transiently or incidentally to some other use of this publication) without the written permission of the copyright owner, except in accordance with the provisions of the Copyright, Designs and Patents Act 1988 or under the terms of a licence issued by the Copyright Licensing Agency, Saffron House, 6–10 Kirby Street, London EC1N 8TS (www.cla.co.uk). Applications for the copyright owner's written permission should be addressed to the publisher.

Edited by Nancy Dickmann and Abby Colich
Designed by Victoria Allen
Original illustrations © 2013
Illustrated by HL Studios
Picture research by Ruth Blair
Originated by Capstone Global Library Limited
Printed and bound in China by CTPS

ISBN 978 1 406 24920 0 (hardback)
16 15 14 13 12
10 9 8 7 6 5 4 3 2 1

ISBN 978 1 406 24927 9 (paperback)
17 16 15 14 13
10 9 8 7 6 5 4 3 2 1

British Library Cataloguing in Publication Data
Waldron, Melanie.
Mapping information. -- (Let's get mapping!)
912-dc23
A full catalogue record for this book is available from the British Library.

Acknowledgements

We would like to thank the following for permission to reproduce photographs: Alamy: p. 9 (© Andrew Aitchison), 25 (© Mim Friday); Corbis: p. 26 (© Kevin Dodge); © Copyright SASI Group (University of Sheffield): p. 24; Shutterstock: pp. 4 (© Thomas La Mela), 5 (© Tom Grundy), 15 (© gemphotography), 17 (© Tarasenko Sergey), 21 (© Pincasso); Superstock: pp. 20 (© Marka), 22 (© Easy-Pix), 23 (© Ron Nickel / Design Pics); USGS: p. 27.

Cover photograph of globe with people reproduced with permission of Alamy (© Robert Matton AB). Cover photograph of girl reproduced with permission of Shutterstock (© Ilike).

Background and design features reproduced with permission from Shutterstock.
Every effort has been made to contact copyright holders of material reproduced in this book. Any omissions will be rectified in subsequent printings if notice is given to the publisher.

All the internet addresses (URLs) given in this book were valid at the time of going to press. However, due to the dynamic nature of the internet, some addresses may have changed, or sites may have changed or ceased to exist since publication. While the author and publisher regret any inconvenience this may cause readers, no responsibility for any such changes can be accepted by either the author or the publisher.

EAST RIDING OF YORKSHIRE SCHOOLS LIBRARY SERVICE	
901186284 8	
Peters Books	20-May-2014
	£7.99

Contents

Some words appear in the text in bold, **like this**. You can find out what they mean by looking in the glossary.

What is a map?

There are lots of different types of maps. Most maps are flat pieces of paper showing information about the land. They might show the buildings and roads on the land. They might show the land's **natural features**, such as hills, mountains, and rivers. They might show other kinds of information, such as the number of people living in an area.

Some parts of the world have huge numbers of people living there. Maps can show where these places are.

Mapping different information

Many maps are really useful for showing how places are different. For example, a map could show the **percentage** of people that can read in a country. You could simply write the number on the map. But you could also use different colours, or **symbols**, to represent different numbers. If you did this for all the countries in the world, you would quickly see some patterns.

Even vast, empty places like this can be measured and mapped. We could measure things such as rainfall or hours of sunshine.

STATISTICAL MAPS

Statistics are simply amounts or numbers of something. For example, the number of tourists visiting a town is a statistic. Maps that show statistics are called statistical maps, or thematic maps.

Changing colours

Some mapmakers use colour to show information about areas on a map. The information can be split into groups and a different shade of colour is used for each group. Each area is then coloured in the correct shade. A **key** can explain what each shade of colour means.

The map below shows information about the time taken for children to travel to school. Areas where average journeys are short (less than five minutes) are shown in blue. Areas where journeys are very long (over 15 minutes) are shown in orange. Areas with journey times in between are shown in different shades of colour.

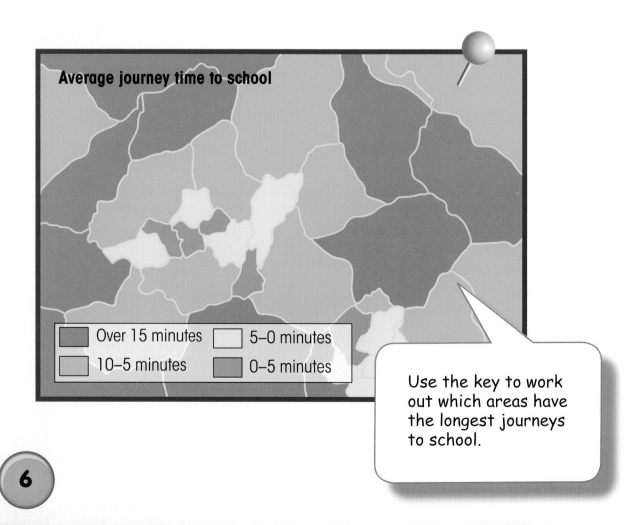

Average journey time to school

| Over 15 minutes | 5–0 minutes |
| 10–5 minutes | 0–5 minutes |

Use the key to work out which areas have the longest journeys to school.

Many colours, many shades

Most coloured maps use different shades of one colour to show different amounts of something. This can help us to pick out patterns in the information. Sometimes darker or lighter shades of one colour will be used to show more or less of something. See the map below for an example of this.

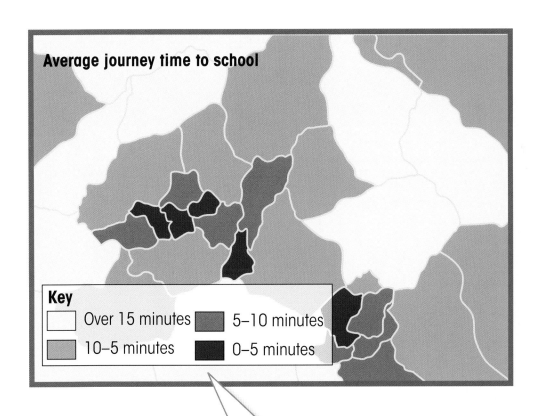

Average journey time to school

Key

- Over 15 minutes
- 10–5 minutes
- 5–10 minutes
- 0–5 minutes

Compare this map with the one on page 6. It is showing the same information, but using different colours. Which map do you think is easiest to understand?

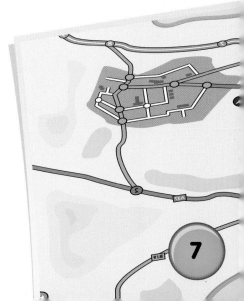

Different scales

Maps shrink the land down to fit in a small area. This is called scaling down. Maps that shrink things down a lot, such as country maps, are called small-scale maps. They show a large area, but there is not much detail. Small-scale maps can show information and patterns about large areas. For example, a world map of average temperatures would show that the coldest areas are near the **North** and **South Poles**.

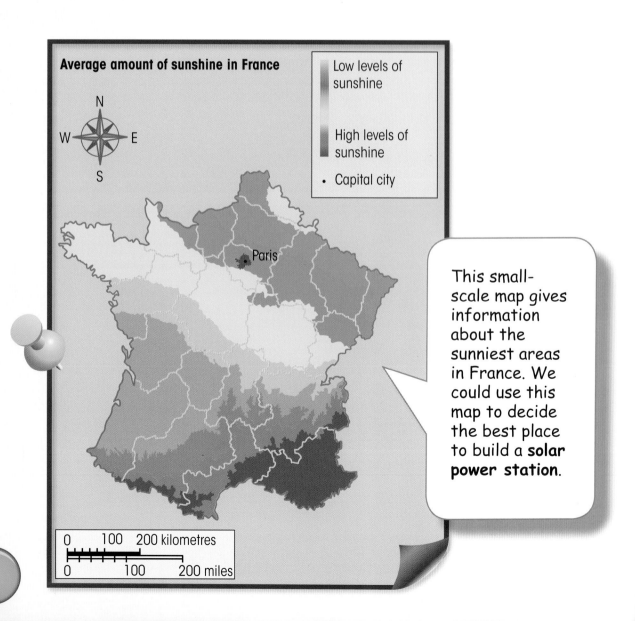

Average amount of sunshine in France

N
W — E
S

Low levels of sunshine

High levels of sunshine

• Capital city

Paris

0   100   200 kilometres

0   100   200 miles

This small-scale map gives information about the sunniest areas in France. We could use this map to decide the best place to build a **solar power station**.

Large-scale maps

Maps that shrink everything down a lot less, such as town maps, are called large-scale maps. They do not show large areas but they can show huge amounts of detail about the land. Maps of buildings, such as hospitals or schools, are very large-scale maps. They can show very detailed information about the building – for example, where the toilets are.

A very large-scale map of this school could show people where to find the classroom they want to visit.

Symbols on maps

Most maps use symbols to show information about places. Symbols are usually little pictures or shapes that represent something. For example, a red cross might represent a hospital. Symbols are helpful for showing information on a map without using words.

The symbols on this map show where each type of natural **resource** can be found.

North
West — East
South

INDIAN OCEAN

SOUTH AFRICA

ATLANTIC OCEAN

KEY

Coal   Gold
Diamonds   Oil
Fishing

FINDING KEYS

Maps that use symbols usually also have a key. A key is a list of the symbols on the map. The key explains what each symbol means. When you look at a map with symbols on it, you should always look at the key so you understand what the map is showing you.

Bigger symbols

Symbols can be used on maps to show different amounts of things. Bigger symbols, or more symbols, mean a larger amount of something. This means that symbols show not only where something is, but also how much is there.

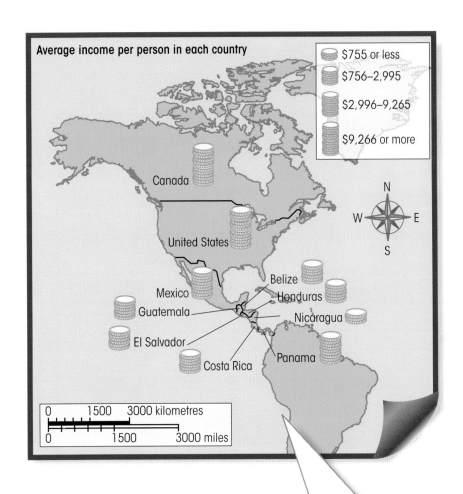

Average income per person in each country

	$755 or less
	$756–2,995
	$2,996–9,265
	$9,266 or more

Canada

United States

Mexico

Guatemala

El Salvador

Costa Rica

Belize

Honduras

Nicaragua

Panama

N W E S

0   1500   3000 kilometres
0   1500   3000 miles

This map of North America shows the average amount that people earn in a year. Tall stacks of coins show wealthy countries and short stacks of coins show less wealthy countries.

Dot maps

Some maps can show where there are groups, or clusters, of things. Mapmakers sometimes use little dots on maps to represent something, or even a large number of things. These are called dot maps. They are very useful for locating large clusters of something.

For example, you could mark a dot for every tree you see in your neighbourhood. If there is a local park with lots of trees, there would be lots of dots there. Your map would show where the clusters of trees are.

In this map of Australia, a dot represents 500 people. You can use this map to see where the heavily populated areas are.

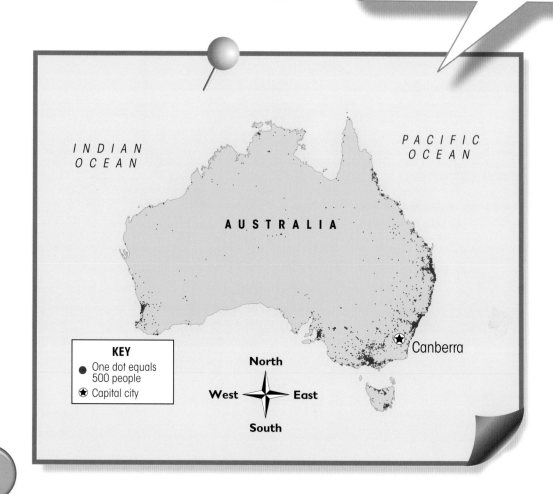

INDIAN OCEAN

PACIFIC OCEAN

AUSTRALIA

★ Canberra

KEY
● One dot equals 500 people
★ Capital city

North
West — East
South

Lots of dots!

Different coloured dots can be used to show different groups of things. For example, if you wanted to make a map of where different animals are found in a nature reserve, you could use a different colour for each type of animal. A lion could be a red dot, an elephant could be a blue dot, and so on. The map would then show clusters of animals across the reserve.

Use the key to work out which types of animal are found across the nature reserve.

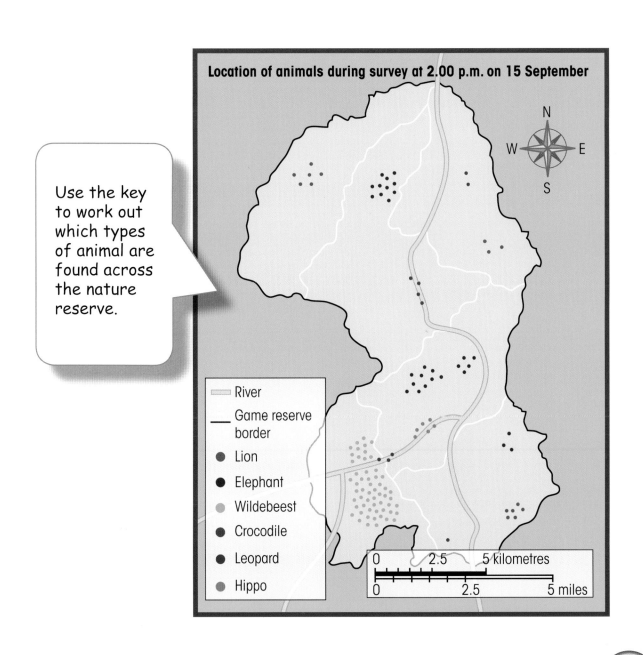

Location of animals during survey at 2.00 p.m. on 15 September

Key:
- River
- Game reserve border
- Lion
- Elephant
- Wildebeest
- Crocodile
- Leopard
- Hippo

0   2.5   5 kilometres
0   2.5   5 miles

Maps showing movement

It is sometimes useful to show the movement of something on a map. You may have seen maps that show the movements of **ocean currents** or winds. But we can also show the movement of things such as goods or tourists.

Some maps use **flow lines** to represent movement of something. Flow lines show where something comes from and goes to. If we wanted to show different amounts, we could use thicker or thinner flow lines to represent these amounts.

This flow line map shows that far more people travel to work from the town to the city. This is shown by a thicker flow line.

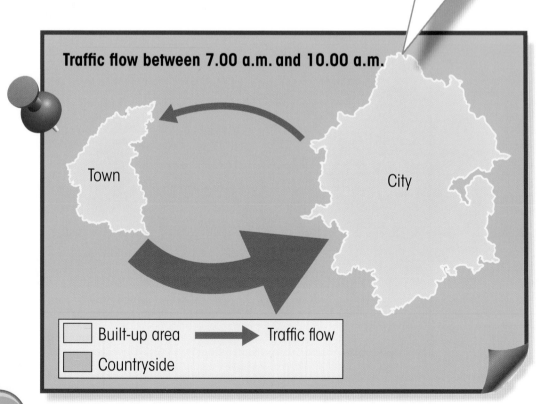

Traffic flow between 7.00 a.m. and 10.00 a.m.

Town

City

Built-up area   → Traffic flow

Countryside

Lots of people travel to work in one direction, and very few in the other direction. Flow line maps can show us this kind of information.

All directions

Flow lines don't have to go in just two directions, forwards and backwards. They can go in all directions to show all the places that something moves to. For example, a map of your country could show flow lines for its exports. A flow line would go from your country to every country that receives exports. The flow lines could be different thicknesses to show that more exports go to some countries.

Maps about history

Maps are not only useful for learning about today. They also help us to understand the past. Lots of historical information can be shown on a map. For example, maps can show the routes that explorers took across oceans and countries. Maps can also show us where historical battles were won and lost.

This map shows the route that Captain Cook sailed when he set out from the UK in 1768.

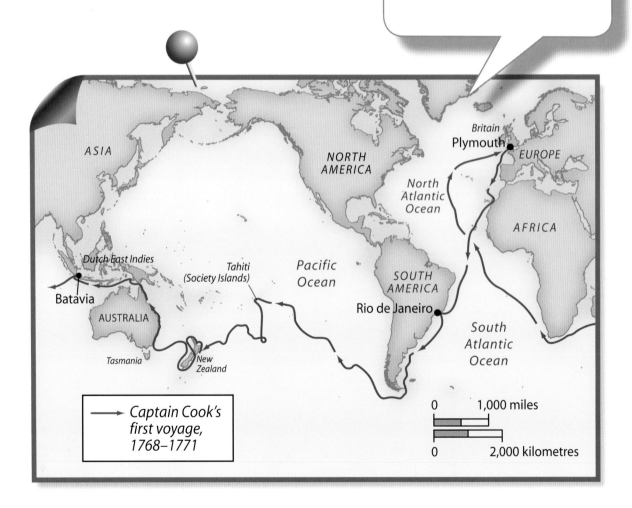

ASIA

NORTH AMERICA

Britain
Plymouth
EUROPE

North Atlantic Ocean

AFRICA

Dutch East Indies

Tahiti (Society Islands)

Pacific Ocean

SOUTH AMERICA

Batavia

AUSTRALIA

Rio de Janeiro

South Atlantic Ocean

Tasmania

New Zealand

→ Captain Cook's first voyage, 1768–1771

0   1,000 miles

0   2,000 kilometres

Maps from the past

People have been making maps for hundreds of years. We know that today's maps are very accurate because we can use **satellite images** and **aerial** photographs to check them. In the past, people simply had to draw maps using sketches of the land.

Some really old maps look very different from today's maps. They were made when people didn't know about the whole of the world. Lots of world maps made by the Romans don't show North America or South America, because they didn't know these lands existed.

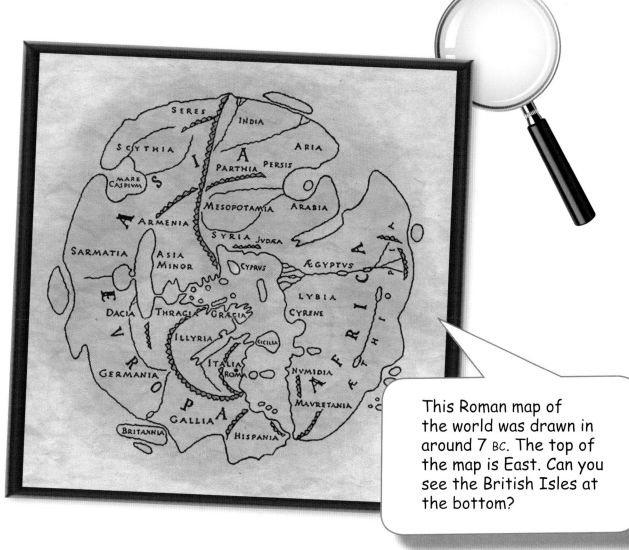

This Roman map of the world was drawn in around 7 BC. The top of the map is East. Can you see the British Isles at the bottom?

Equal lines and time zones

It is sometimes useful to see on a map where things are the same. Where lots of places have the same amount of something, such as rainfall, we can join up these points with lines. Lines that join equal points are called **isolines**.

For example, you could mark distance isolines on a map of your school and the local area. You could draw a circle on the map to show everything that is 1 kilometre from your school. You could then draw more circles, at 2 kilometres, 3 kilometres, and so on.

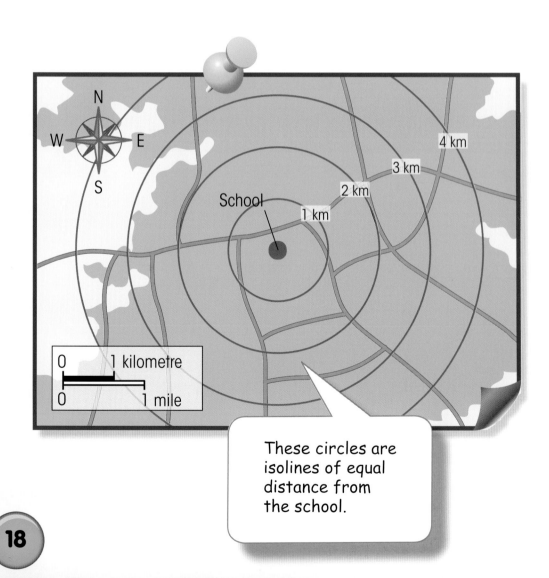

These circles are isolines of equal distance from the school.

Time zones

Across the world, the time of day is different. World maps can show all the different time zones on a map. These are areas where the time is the same. You can use a time-zone map to work out what the time will be in another country.

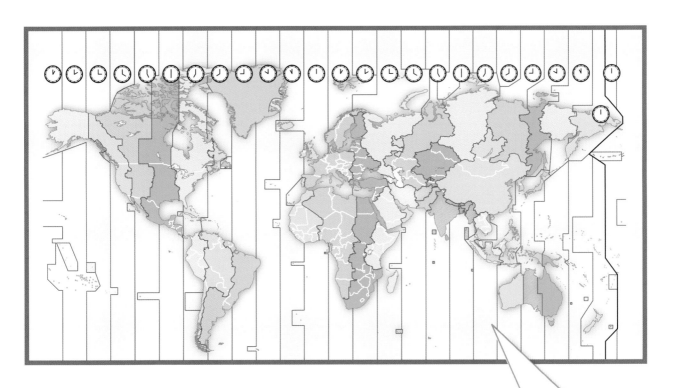

MANY TIME ZONES

Some time-zone lines are "bent" to follow a country's **border**, so that the time is the same across the country. Large countries, such as the United States, need to have several time zones.

Moving one zone to the East adds one hour to the time. Moving one zone to the West takes away one hour from the time.

Online maps

Today, there are thousands of maps that are free to explore and use. The internet has several mapping websites where you can simply enter a place name or a postcode. The map of your chosen area will come onto the screen. You can then zoom in or out, and move the map to new areas.

You can also search for certain things, such as cinemas. The map can show your area with all the cinemas marked on it. Online maps can show huge amounts of useful information like this.

It is so easy to find places using online maps. Have a go!

Planning journeys

Online maps make it really easy to plan journeys. They can work out the best route and tell you the time you will need to travel. They can show this information on the map, and they also usually list instructions, such as "turn left on the High Street".

SATNAV SYSTEMS

Once you are travelling, **satnav** systems can help to stop you from getting lost! **Satellites** can send signals to cars and mobile phones with satnav systems. These can then work out where you are on their maps, and can direct you to where you need to go.

Exit 64 right

50 MPH

Arrival 2:00 PM

Menu

Turn In 2 miles

Changing maps

Some **digital maps** show changing information. They are very useful for people like fishermen. Fishing boats can send out **sonar signals** to help locate fish. The digital maps show where the fish are. The maps are always updating and changing as the fish swim around.

Fishers use sonar signals to help them locate fish.

WATCHING THE WEATHER

Digital weather maps can also show changing information. Many people out walking in mountainous areas need up-to-date weather maps to make sure that they do not get caught out in bad storms.

High-tech farming

Some farmers use digital maps to help them. Many modern tractors are fitted with satnav systems. These can guide the tractors up and down fields in perfectly straight lines. Before, farmers had to concentrate all the time to make sure they were ploughing in straight lines. Now, they can take their hands off the wheel and let the satnav do the steering! The maps update and change as the tractor moves, keeping it on track.

This farmer uses satnav technology in her combine.

Strange maps

Some maps show information by changing the shape and size of the land! The size of an area of land is changed depending on the statistic for that area. A map of the world could show the population of each country in this way. A country with a large population, such as China, would be shown as a huge area. Maps that show information in this way are called **cartograms**.

Compare this map with a standard world map. Australia has a small population, so it is much smaller on this map.

Squashed and stretched

Many transport maps, such as train maps, are made much simpler than in real life. Railway lines are straightened. Stations are spaced out more evenly. This makes the maps easier to read and understand. They only show the information you need, for example, which railway lines connect together and which stations they stop at. You don't really need to know the exact distances.

THE LONDON UNDERGROUND MAP

In 1933, a new map of the London Underground was made. People did not like the map at first because it was not geographically correct. However, many transport maps around the world are now based on it.

Making statistical maps

Making statistical maps is a bit different from making other types of maps. Usually you will use a "base map" of an area that shows only the borders between countries or regions. The rest of the map is left blank for you to fill in with the information you are interested in.

You can use shades of colour, different colours, dots, symbols, or lines to show information on a map. It depends on the information you want to show.

Geographical information systems

A **geographical information system**, or GIS, is a computer system that holds lots of different information. All of the information is linked to a place on a map. The information could be about anything – weather, soil type, population, traffic, or buildings – as long as it is linked to a place.

When using a GIS, people first need to decide what information they are interested in. Then they can get the computer to plot that information on a map. There might be only one layer of information, or lots of different layers! A GIS can compare the information in different layers.

This image shows some of the layers of information that can go into a GIS.

Get mapping!

Why not try making your own geographical information system? Your classmates or teacher can help you find the information you need.

1) First, make a blank "base map" of your school. Your school office may already have something like this. Make sure it shows all the classrooms.

2) Now use tracing paper to make layers of information for your GIS. Each layer could show a different type of information, for example:

- number of pupils in each classroom
- average age of pupils in each classroom
- average height of pupils in each classroom
- dots for every five pupils to show where people go at break time.

3) For each layer, decide which type of map would be best. Do you want to use shades of colour? Do you want to make a dot map? If you want to use shades of colour, decide which colours would be best.

4) Finally, you can insert all the layers into a file with the base map at the bottom. You now have your own GIS!

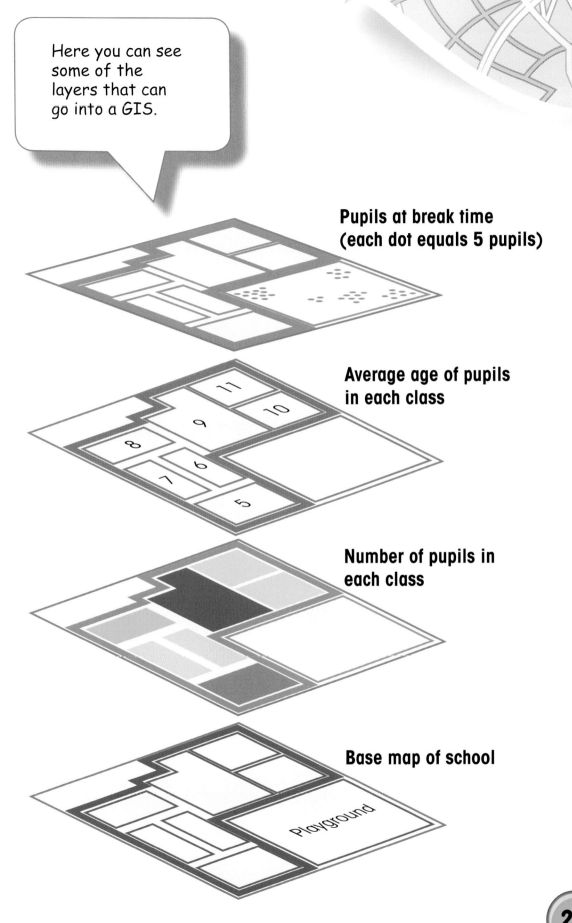

Here you can see some of the layers that can go into a GIS.

Pupils at break time (each dot equals 5 pupils)

Average age of pupils in each class

Number of pupils in each class

Base map of school

Playground

Glossary

aerial high above ground

border imaginary line that separates different countries, or different regions inside a country

cartogram map that changes the size and shape of countries as a way of showing information about each country

digital map map that is shown on a screen such as a computer or a mobile phone

flow lines lines on a map that can show the movement of something

geographical information system computer system with lots of different layers of information

isoline line joining points that are equal in some way

key list of symbols and an explanation of what each one represents

natural feature something on Earth's surface that has been created by nature, for example a mountain

North Pole world's northernmost tip

ocean current huge body of sea water that flows in the same direction; it can be warm or cold

percentage amount of something that is represented as a portion of 100 per cent

resource something that is of value to humans that Earth can provide

satellite spacecraft that travels around Earth and gathers or sends back information

satellite image picture, like a photograph, that a satellite can take of Earth from space

satnav short for "satellite navigation", which means using signals from satellites to help us find our location

solar power station building that captures energy from the Sun's rays and turns it into electricity

sonar signal sonar is short for "sound navigation and ranging"; a sonar signal is a sound signal that is used to find objects underwater

South Pole world's southernmost tip

symbol object or a picture that represents something

Find out more

There is a whole world of maps and mapping waiting to be discovered! Begin by looking at these books and websites.

Books

Introducing Maps (Maps and Mapping Skills), Meg and Jack Gillett (Wayland, 2010)

Map Types (All Over the Map), Kate Torpie (Crabtree Publishing, 2008)

The Once Upon a Time Map Book, B. G. Hennessey and Peter Joyce (Candlewick Press, 2010)

Using Maps (Ways Into Geography), Claire Llewellyn (Franklin Watts, 2009)

Websites

earthpulse.nationalgeographic.com/earthpulse/earthpulse-map
On this website, you can see a lot of different geographical information on a world map. Simply click on the layer of information you are interested in, in the list on the left, and the map will show the information.

maps.google.co.uk
Here you can find maps of any area in the world. You can zoom in and out, and you can view land from the ground.

mapzone.ordnancesurvey.co.uk/mapzone/index.html
This is an interactive site all about maps and mapping, with homework help, maps, photos, and games. The teaching resources section includes lots of useful sheets about map skills.

www.worldmapper.org
Worldmapper has lots of maps where countries are sized differently! All the maps show some statistics, with some very strange-looking maps indeed.

Index